DID YOU EVER WONDER...

For years I have been collecting these ridiculous yet thought provoking questions from all over the internet, television commercials, and from my students. Most of them have been reproduced for decades so it is impossible to give credit to their original sources. My 5th grade students walk into the classroom with a new *Did you ever wonder...* written on the board each morning. These questions have sparked many interesting conversations to start off the day. Use this book as a start to your work day, as a header on your e-mails, as a question to pose to your co-workers, as an ice breaker, or for your own enjoyment. I cannot take credit for creating all of them (although many are original), but I can provide you with this collection that will keep you wondering for years to come.

DID YOU EVER WONDER...

If corn oil comes from corn, where does baby oil come from?

DID YOU EVER WONDER...

If a picture is worth a thousand words, what is a picture of a thousand words worth?

DID YOU EVER WONDER...

What do people in China call their good plates?

Did You Ever Wonder....

OVER **250** IDIOTIC AND MIND NUMBING
QUESTIONS TO PONDER

Brendan D. Lynch

1776 PRESS

1776 Press
19 Coleman Road
Suite #105
Wethersfield, CT 06109

DID YOU EVER WONDER...

First Edition © 2005
ISBN 1-4116-2361-4

Second Edition © 2010
ISBN 978-0-9825243-0-5

Cover Design by KnockMedia
www.knockmedia.com

Editing by Levine Editorial Services

Printed in the United States of America

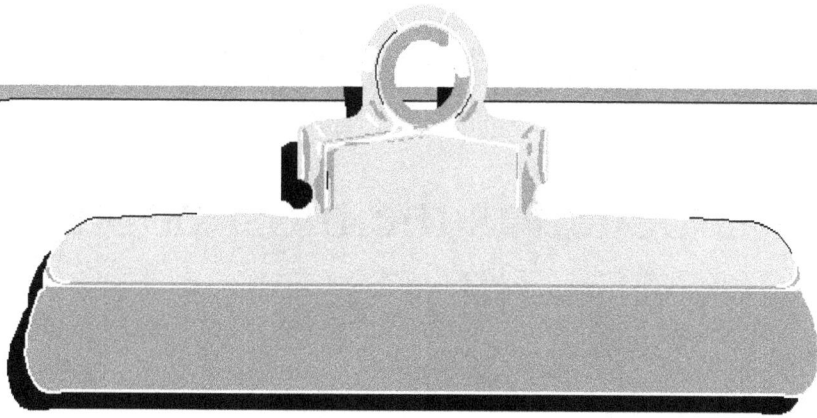

This book is dedicated to

my 5th grade students at

Thompson Brook School

DID YOU EVER WONDER...

If the #2 pencil is the most popular,
then why is it still #2?

DID YOU EVER WONDER...

How much deeper would the ocean be
if sponges didn't grow in it?

DID YOU EVER WONDER...

If anything is possible, then is it
possible that nothing is possible?

DID YOU EVER WONDER...

Is it true that cannibals don't eat clowns because they taste funny?

DID YOU EVER WONDER...

Why is "abbreviated" such a long word?

DID YOU EVER WONDER...

Can fat people go skinny-dipping?

DID YOU EVER WONDER...

Is a man full of wonder a wonderful man?

DID YOU EVER WONDER...

Is a hot car cool or is a cool car hot?

DID YOU EVER WONDER...

If electricity comes from electrons, does morality come from morons?

3

DID YOU EVER WONDER...

Why do you get on a bus or a train but get into a car?

DID YOU EVER WONDER...

Why are they called apartments when they are all stuck together?

DID YOU EVER WONDER...

Why do you ask someone without a watch what time it is?

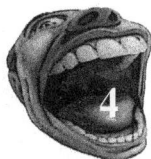

4

DID YOU EVER WONDER...

Why does sour cream have an expiration date?

DID YOU EVER WONDER...

The light went out, but where did they go?

DID YOU EVER WONDER...

Why do banks charge you an "insufficient funds" fee on money they already know that you don't have?

5

DID YOU EVER WONDER...

Does the reverse side also have a reverse side?

DID YOU EVER WONDER...

If the universe is everything, and scientists say that the universe is expanding, what is it expanding into?

DID YOU EVER WONDER...

If you got into a taxi and the driver started driving backwards, would the taxi driver end up owing you money?

DID YOU EVER WONDER...

If a tree falls in the forest and no one is around to see it, do the other trees make fun of it?

DID YOU EVER WONDER...

Do fish get cramps after eating?

DID YOU EVER WONDER...

Why are there five syllables in "monosyllabic"?

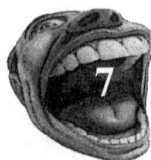

DID YOU EVER WONDER...

Why do they call it the Department of Interior when they are in charge of everything outside?

DID YOU EVER WONDER...

If vegetarians eat vegetables, what do humanitarians eat?

DID YOU EVER WONDER...

When you erase a word with a pencil, where does it go?

DID YOU EVER WONDER...

When a door is open it is ajar, so when a jar is open shouldn't it be a door?

DID YOU EVER WONDER...

Why buy a product that takes 2000 flushes to get rid of?

DID YOU EVER WONDER...

What happens if someone loses a lost and found box?

DID YOU EVER WONDER...

What if the hokey pokey really is what it's all about?

DID YOU EVER WONDER...

What's the difference between a wise man and a wise guy?

DID YOU EVER WONDER...

How can you hear yourself think?

DID YOU EVER WONDER...

Why do we wash bath towels? Aren't we clean when we use them?

DID YOU EVER WONDER...

Why do we put suits in a garment bag and put garments in a suitcase?

DID YOU EVER WONDER...

Why doesn't glue stick to the inside of the bottle?

DID YOU EVER WONDER...

Do Roman paramedics refer to "IV's" as "4's"?

DID YOU EVER WONDER...

What do little birdies see when they get knocked unconscious?

DID YOU EVER WONDER...

Why doesn't Tarzan have a beard?

DID YOU EVER WONDER...

If man evolved from monkeys and apes, why do we still have monkeys and apes?

DID YOU EVER WONDER...

Is Disney World a people trap operated by a mouse?

DID YOU EVER WONDER...

Isn't the best way to save face to keep the lower part shut?

DID YOU EVER WONDER...

Before they invented drawing boards, what did they go back to?

DID YOU EVER WONDER...

How do you set your laser printer on stun?

DID YOU EVER WONDER...

How is it possible to have a "civil" war?

DID YOU EVER WONDER...

If all of the world is a stage, where is the audience sitting?

DID YOU EVER WONDER...

If one synchronized swimmer drowns, do the rest have to drown too?

DID YOU EVER WONDER...

How do "Keep Off the Grass" signs get on the grass in the first place?

15

DID YOU EVER WONDER...

If you ate pasta and antipasto, would you still be hungry?

DID YOU EVER WONDER...

If you try to fail, and succeed, which have you done?

DID YOU EVER WONDER...

Is a castrated pig disgruntled?

DID YOU EVER WONDER...

If most car accidents occur within five miles of home, why doesn't everyone just move 6 miles away?

DID YOU EVER WONDER...

Why is the alphabet in that order? Is it because of that song?

DID YOU EVER WONDER...

What happens when none of your bees wax?

DID YOU EVER WONDER...

If the black box flight recorder is never damaged during a plane crash, why isn't the whole airplane made out of the same stuff?

DID YOU EVER WONDER...

Why is it called tourist season if you can't shoot at them?

DID YOU EVER WONDER...

If all those psychics know the winning lottery numbers, why are they all still working?

DID YOU EVER WONDER...

Could it be that all those trick-or-treaters wearing sheets aren't going as ghosts but as mattresses?

DID YOU EVER WONDER...

If a mute swears, does his mother wash his hands with soap?

DID YOU EVER WONDER...

Whose cruel idea was it for the word "lisp" to have an "s" in it?

DID YOU EVER WONDER...

If someone with multiple personalities threatens to kill himself, is it considered a hostage situation?

DID YOU EVER WONDER...

Is there another word for synonym?

DID YOU EVER WONDER...

Why do doctors call what they do "practice"?

DID YOU EVER WONDER...

When sign makers go on strike, is anything written on their signs?

DID YOU EVER WONDER...

Where do forest rangers go when they want to get away and take a camping trip?

DID YOU EVER WONDER...

Why isn't there mouse-flavored cat food?

DID YOU EVER WONDER...

Why do they report power outages on TV?

DID YOU EVER WONDER...

What do you do when you see an endangered animal eating an endangered plant?

DID YOU EVER WONDER...

Is it possible to be totally partial?

DID YOU EVER WONDER...

What's another word for thesaurus?

DID YOU EVER WONDER...

If a parsley farmer is sued, can they garnish his wages?

DID YOU EVER WONDER...

Would a fly without wings be called a walk?

DID YOU EVER WONDER...

Why do they lock gas station bathrooms? Are they afraid someone will clean them?

DID YOU EVER WONDER...

Why do people who know the least know it the loudest?

DID YOU EVER WONDER...

If the funeral procession is at night, do folks drive with their headlights off?

DID YOU EVER WONDER...

If a stealth bomber crashes in a forest, will it make a sound?

DID YOU EVER WONDER...

If a turtle doesn't have a shell, is he homeless or naked?

DID YOU EVER WONDER...

Why do they call it a black light when it's really purple?

25

DID YOU EVER WONDER...

Is a sleeping bag a nap sack?

DID YOU EVER WONDER...

What came first, the fruit or the color orange?

DID YOU EVER WONDER...

If there's an exception to every rule, is there an exception to that rule?

26

DID YOU EVER WONDER...

Why is it called lipstick when it always comes off?

DID YOU EVER WONDER...

Do sheep shrink when they get wet?

DID YOU EVER WONDER...

Should vegetarians eat animal crackers?

27

DID YOU EVER WONDER...

If the cops arrest a mime, do they tell him he has the right to remain silent?

DID YOU EVER WONDER...

When companies ship Styrofoam, what do they pack it in?

DID YOU EVER WONDER...

If you're cross-eyed and have dyslexia, can you read normally?

DID YOU EVER WONDER...

If you throw a cat out a car window does it become Kitty Litter?

DID YOU EVER WONDER...

If corn oil comes from corn, where does baby oil come from?

DID YOU EVER WONDER...

How do they get deer to cross at that yellow road sign?

DID YOU EVER WONDER...

Why do they sterilize the needles for lethal injections?

DID YOU EVER WONDER...

Why do kamikaze pilots wear helmets?

DID YOU EVER WONDER...

Why do psychics have to ask you for your name?

DID YOU EVER WONDER...

Is it true that cannibals don't eat clowns because they taste funny?

DID YOU EVER WONDER...

Do blind Eskimos have Seeing Eye sled dogs?

DID YOU EVER WONDER...

If a deaf person has to go to court, is it still called a hearing?

31

DID YOU EVER WONDER...

Why do they call it a TV set when you only get one?

DID YOU EVER WONDER...

Do radioactive cats have 18 half-lives?

DID YOU EVER WONDER...

Why is it when you transport something by car it's called a shipment, but when you transport by ship it's called a cargo?

DID YOU EVER WONDER...

If you shoot a mime, should you use a silencer?

DID YOU EVER WONDER...

What was the best thing before sliced bread?

DID YOU EVER WONDER...

Why does the sun lighten our hair, but darken our skin?

33

DID YOU EVER WONDER...

Why can't women put on mascara with their mouth closed?

DID YOU EVER WONDER...

Can a hearse carrying a corpse drive in the carpool lane?

DID YOU EVER WONDER...

Why is it that no matter what color of bubble bath you use the bubbles are always white?

DID YOU EVER WONDER...

Why don't you ever see the headline "Psychic Wins Lottery"?

DID YOU EVER WONDER...

Why is a boxing ring square?

DID YOU EVER WONDER...

What would the speed of lightning be if it didn't zigzag?

DID YOU EVER WONDER...

Why is it called lipstick if you can still move your lips?

DID YOU EVER WONDER...

Why is it considered necessary to nail down the lid of a coffin?

DID YOU EVER WONDER...

If money doesn't grow on trees then why do banks have branches?

DID YOU EVER WONDER...

Why is it that rain drops, but snow falls?

DID YOU EVER WONDER...

Why is it that to stop Windows, you have to click on "Start"?

DID YOU EVER WONDER...

Why is it that people say they "slept like a baby" when babies wake up every couple of hours?

DID YOU EVER WONDER...

Why is it that when you're driving and looking for an address, you turn down the volume on the radio?

DID YOU EVER WONDER...

Why is lemon juice made with artificial flavor, and dishwashing liquid made with real lemons?

DID YOU EVER WONDER...

Why is the man who invests all of your money called a broker?

38

DID YOU EVER WONDER...

Why is the third hand on a watch called the second hand?

DID YOU EVER WONDER...

Why is the time of day with the slowest traffic called rush hour?

DID YOU EVER WONDER...

Why are you in a movie, but on TV?

DID YOU EVER WONDER...

What disease did cured ham actually have?

DID YOU EVER WONDER...

Why isn't there a special name for the tops of your feet?

DID YOU EVER WONDER...

When you close your eyes, do you see nothing or do you see the color black?

DID YOU EVER WONDER...

Can atheists get insurance for Acts of God?

DID YOU EVER WONDER...

Can you be arrested for running into a firehouse and yelling, "Movie! Movie!"?

DID YOU EVER WONDER...

How do you know when you're out of invisible ink?

41

DID YOU EVER WONDER...

If a cat always lands on its feet, and buttered bread always lands butter side down, what would happen if you tied buttered bread to the top of a cat?

DID YOU EVER WONDER...

If Jimmy cracks corn and no one cares, why does he keep doing it?

DID YOU EVER WONDER...

If knees were backwards, what would chairs look like?

DID YOU EVER WONDER...

If pro is the opposite of con, is progress the opposite of congress?

DID YOU EVER WONDER...

If quitters never win, and winners never quit, then why quit while you're ahead?

DID YOU EVER WONDER...

Why do we drive on parkways and park on driveways?

DID YOU EVER WONDER...

Why do buffalo wings taste like chicken?

DID YOU EVER WONDER...

Why do they call them "free gifts"? Aren't all gifts free?

DID YOU EVER WONDER...

If a cow laughed hard, would milk come out of her nose?

DID YOU EVER WONDER...

Why isn't the number 11 pronounced onety-one?

DID YOU EVER WONDER...

How important does a person have to be before they are considered assassinated instead of just murdered?

DID YOU EVER WONDER...

If a 911 operator has a heart attack, whom does she call?

45

DID YOU EVER WONDER...

Why do people pay to go up tall buildings and then put money into binoculars to look at things on the ground?

DID YOU EVER WONDER...

Do fish ever drink water?

DID YOU EVER WONDER...

Why does a round pizza come in a square box?

46

DID YOU EVER WONDER...

How is it that we put a man on the moon before we figured out it would be a good idea to put wheels on luggage?

DID YOU EVER WONDER...

If we're here to help other people, what are the other people here for?

DID YOU EVER WONDER...

Why is it called "after dark" when it is really "after light"?

DID YOU EVER WONDER...

Is it good if a vacuum really sucks?

DID YOU EVER WONDER...

Why do we say, "something is out of whack?" What is a whack?

DID YOU EVER WONDER...

Why do "tug" boats "push" their barges?

DID YOU EVER WONDER...

Why don't you ever see a toad on a toadstool?

DID YOU EVER WONDER...

If you spend your day doing nothing, how do you know when you're done?

DID YOU EVER WONDER...

If it is zero degrees outside today, and it is supposed to be twice as cold tomorrow, how cold is it going to be?

DID YOU EVER WONDER...

If you steal a clean slate, does it go on your record?

DID YOU EVER WONDER...

What do sheep count when they can't sleep?

DID YOU EVER WONDER...

What happened to the first six ups?

DID YOU EVER WONDER...

If we call each other a chicken when we are afraid, what do chickens call each other when they are afraid?

DID YOU EVER WONDER...

What happens if you get scared half to death twice?

DID YOU EVER WONDER...

Why do bars advertise live bands?

51

DID YOU EVER WONDER...

Why is a person who plays the piano called a pianist, but a person who drives a race car not called a racist?

DID YOU EVER WONDER...

If a fly eats butter does it turn into a butterfly?

DID YOU EVER WONDER...

Why do psychics have to ask you for your name?

DID YOU EVER WONDER...

Is it ok to listen to the AM radio after noon?

DID YOU EVER WONDER...

What do chickens think we taste like?

DID YOU EVER WONDER...

What does Geronimo yell when he jumps out of a plane?

DID YOU EVER WONDER...

Why is an airplane's black box called a "black box" when it is really orange?

DID YOU EVER WONDER...

What do people in China call their good plates?

DID YOU EVER WONDER...

If you got into a taxi and the driver started driving backwards, would the taxi driver end up owing you money?

DID YOU EVER WONDER...

Should you trust a stockbroker who is married to a travel agent?

DID YOU EVER WONDER...

What do you call a male ladybug?

DID YOU EVER WONDER...

What hair color do they put on the driver's license of a bald man?

DID YOU EVER WONDER...

What color is a chameleon on a mirror?

DID YOU EVER WONDER...

Why didn't Noah swat those two mosquitoes?

DID YOU EVER WONDER...

Why are they called safety pins when they are extremely sharp?

DID YOU EVER WONDER...

Why does your nose run and your feet smell?

DID YOU EVER WONDER...

Why does an alarm clock "go off" when it begins ringing?

DID YOU EVER WONDER...

Why do we sing "Take me out to the ball game" when we're already there?

DID YOU EVER WONDER...

Why are they called "stands" when they're made for sitting?

DID YOU EVER WONDER...

Why does "fat chance" and "slim chance" mean the same?

DID YOU EVER WONDER...

Why does "slow down" and "slow up" mean the same?

DID YOU EVER WONDER...

Why do croutons come in airtight packages when it's just stale bread to begin with?

DID YOU EVER WONDER...

If people from Poland are called "Poles", why aren't people from Holland called "Holes"?

DID YOU EVER WONDER...

Do employees at tea companies ever take coffee breaks?

DID YOU EVER WONDER...

Why women can't remember to leave the lid up?

DID YOU EVER WONDER...

How does the guy who drives the snowplow get to work?

DID YOU EVER WONDER...

If there is a daddy-longlegs is there a mommy-longlegs?

DID YOU EVER WONDER...

Can you imagine a world with no hypothetical situations?

DID YOU EVER WONDER...

Why isn't phonetic spelled the way it sounds?

DID YOU EVER WONDER...

What's the difference between null and void?

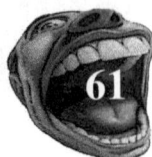

DID YOU EVER WONDER...

What is a female mailman called?

DID YOU EVER WONDER...

Can you cry underwater?

DID YOU EVER WONDER...

Why is it good to be a daddy's girl, but bad to be a momma's boy?

DID YOU EVER WONDER...

If you get cheated by the Better Business Bureau, to whom do you complain?

DID YOU EVER WONDER...

What would Cheese say if he got his picture taken?

DID YOU EVER WONDER...

If Barbie is so popular, then why do you have to buy her friends?

63

DID YOU EVER WONDER...

What do batteries run on?

DID YOU EVER WONDER...

If someone was absent for a test about makeup, would the retake be called a makeup makeup test?

DID YOU EVER WONDER...

What is the speed of dark?

DID YOU EVER WONDER...

How come you never hear about gruntled employees?

DID YOU EVER WONDER...

Why do we choose from only two people for President and 50 people for Miss America?

DID YOU EVER WONDER...

Does a tongue twister actually twist your tongue?

DID YOU EVER WONDER...

Can you be a closet claustrophobic?

DID YOU EVER WONDER...

If a book about failures doesn't sell, is it a success?

DID YOU EVER WONDER...

Do cemetery workers prefer the graveyard shift?

66

DID YOU EVER WONDER...

If a tin whistle is made out of tin, what is a fog horn made out of?

DID YOU EVER WONDER...

Why are there Braille signs on drive-up ATM's?

DID YOU EVER WONDER...

How can there be self-help groups?

DID YOU EVER WONDER...

Why do we play in recitals and recite in plays?

DID YOU EVER WONDER...

Why are there interstate highways in Hawaii?

DID YOU EVER WONDER...

Why are there flotation devices under plane seats instead of parachutes?

DID YOU EVER WONDER...

If a store is open 24 hours a day, 365 days a year, why are there locks on the doors?

DID YOU EVER WONDER...

If nothing sticks to Teflon, how do them make Teflon stick to frying pans?

DID YOU EVER WONDER...

If fire fighters fight fire and crime fighters fight crime, what do freedom fighters fight?

DID YOU EVER WONDER...

Do fish ever get thirsty?

DID YOU EVER WONDER...

If you stick on stickers on a non-stick pan, would they stick on?

DID YOU EVER WONDER...

Why don't ducks duck when you shoot at them?

DID YOU EVER WONDER...

Why does breaking a mirror mean seven years of bad luck when seven is a lucky number?

DID YOU EVER WONDER...

Can angels eat devil's-food cake?

DID YOU EVER WONDER...

If I think, and therefore I am, am I just a thought?

DID YOU EVER WONDER...

If ignorance is bliss, why aren't more people happy?

DID YOU EVER WONDER...

Is it possible to do stand-up comedy sitting down?

DID YOU EVER WONDER...

Is bad a bad word?

DID YOU EVER WONDER...

If dinosaurs had sores, what would they be called?

DID YOU EVER WONDER...

Do bald men wash their heads with soap or shampoo?

DID YOU EVER WONDER...

How can someone be dirt poor, and another be filthy rich?

DID YOU EVER WONDER...

What would happen if you put a humidifier and dehumidifier in the same room?

DID YOU EVER WONDER...

Are one handed people offended when the police tell them to put their hands up?

DID YOU EVER WONDER...

How can sweet and sour sauce be sweet and sour at the same time?

DID YOU EVER WONDER...

If a picture is worth a thousand words, what is a picture of a thousand words worth?

DID YOU EVER WONDER...

If rabbits' feet are so lucky, then what happened to the rabbit?

DID YOU EVER WONDER...

If your plan is having no plan, do you have a plan?

75

DID YOU EVER WONDER...

Do pigs ever pull ham strings?

DID YOU EVER WONDER...

Can dogs have dog days?

DID YOU EVER WONDER...

How do you throw away a garbage can?

76

DID YOU EVER WONDER...

Why are things typed up, but written down?

DID YOU EVER WONDER...

Why do we say "bye-bye," but not "hi-hi?"

DID YOU EVER WONDER...

If you decide that you're indecisive, which one are you?

DID YOU EVER WONDER...

Why do they call it a "running back" when he's running forward?

DID YOU EVER WONDER...

Why do we put suits in a garment bag and put garments in a suitcase?

DID YOU EVER WONDER...

How did the headless horseman know where he was going?

DID YOU EVER WONDER...

How fast do hotcakes sell?

DID YOU EVER WONDER...

If someone can't see, they're blind, and if someone can't hear, they're deaf, so what do we call people who can't smell?

DID YOU EVER WONDER...

Why do we wait until a pig is dead to "cure" it?

DID YOU EVER WONDER...

Why are semi-trucks bigger than regular trucks?

DID YOU EVER WONDER...

If you wore a Teflon suit, could you ever end up in a sticky situation?

DID YOU EVER WONDER...

Why is the word "miniscule" bigger than the word "huge"?

DID YOU EVER WONDER...

Why do scientists call it research when looking for something new?

DID YOU EVER WONDER...

Why don't dogs bark at us when we're talking too loud?

DID YOU EVER WONDER...

Has a snake ever died from a human bite?

81

DID YOU EVER WONDER...

Why is it called a "drive through" if you have to stop?

DID YOU EVER WONDER...

Do geese get people bumps?

DID YOU EVER WONDER...

If you stole a pen from a bank would it be a bank robbery?

DID YOU EVER WONDER...

Is French kissing in France just called kissing?

DID YOU EVER WONDER...

If Canadian bacon is just like ham, is Canadian ham just like bacon?

DID YOU EVER WONDER...

Why is it called pineapple, when there's neither pine nor apple in it?

DID YOU EVER WONDER...

Why do you dust things that are dusty?

DID YOU EVER WONDER...

Can good looking Eskimo girls be called hot?

DID YOU EVER WONDER...

Why is an elevator still called an elevator when it's going down?

84

DID YOU EVER WONDER...

Why is an electrical outlet called an outlet when you plug things into it? Shouldn't it be called an inlet?

DID YOU EVER WONDER...

If practice makes perfect, and nobody's perfect, then why practice?

DID YOU EVER WONDER...

What came first, the chicken or the egg?

ABOUT THE AUTHOR

Brendan Lynch is a 5th grade teacher at Thompson Brook School in Avon, CT. He received a bachelor's degree in English/Creative Writing from the University of Connecticut and his master's degree from Southern Connecticut State University. He currently lives in Connecticut with his wife and son.

www.ingramcontent.com/pod-product-compliance
Lightning Source LLC
Chambersburg PA
CBHW081150040426
42445CB00015B/1829